Living in Space

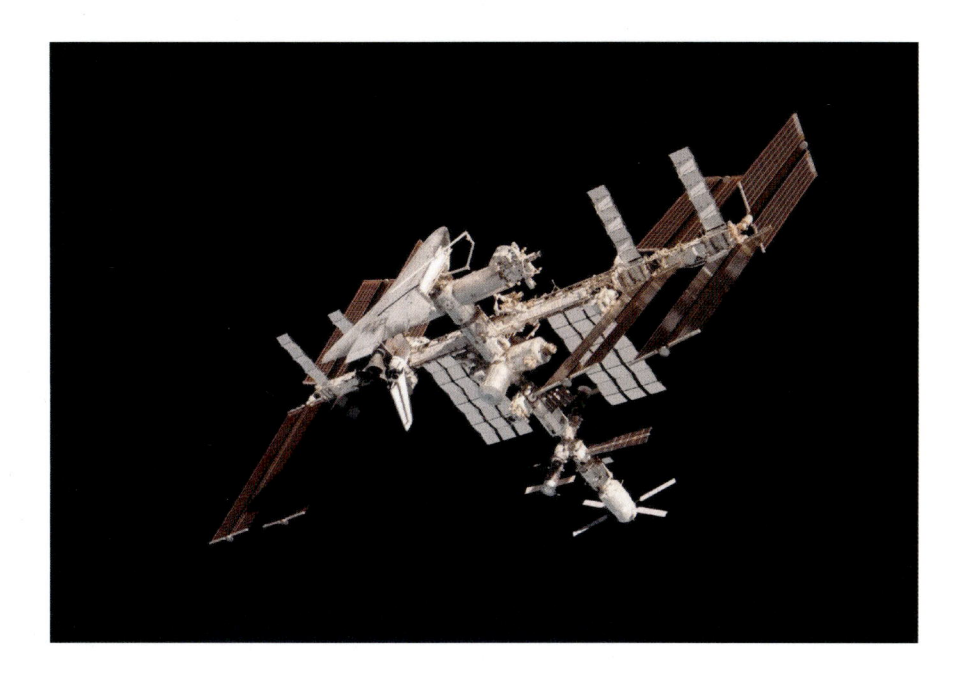

A Kids Book
About Life on the
International Space Station

By Dee Phillips

Living in Space
A Kids Book About Life on the
International Space Station

Published by Dee Phillips
Copyright © 2019 Dee Phillips
Landmark Press Publishing. All rights reserved.
No part of this publication may be reproduced, stored in a retrieval system or transmitted in any form or by any means, electronic, mechanical, photocopy, recording or otherwise, without the written permission of the author.

If you were an astronaut, you could be one of the lucky ones to be chosen to live on a space station. It takes a special person to be an astronaut and it takes a special astronaut to be able to live in space. Living in space on a space station is not like living on Earth. There are many things that you have to be able to do and put up with to be able to survive in space. But if you love space and space travel, it would be wonderful.

International Space Station

You may live on the International Space Station. The International Space Station is the biggest object ever flown in space. The station has been under construction since 1998 when the first piece of the structure was launched into orbit - which was the Zarva Control Module. In 2008 the science lab Columbus was added to the station. That increased the structure to eight rooms.

Astronauts Aboard Expedition 1

The Expedition 1 brought the first crew members to the International Space Station. It was launched October 31, 2000. It docked on November 2, 2000. The space station has been visited by 204 individuals. November 2nd, 2010 marked the 10th anniversary of continuous human occupation.

To give you an idea of the size of the International Space Station, it's module length is 167.3 feet with a habitable volume of 388 cubic meters (or 13,696 cubic feet). In total, it is 357 feet long from end to end, which is about the length of a football field, including the end zones. It is larger than a six bedroom house. It is almost four times as large as the Russian space station, Mir, and about five times as large as the U.S. Skylab. The solar array wingspan on the International Space Station is 240 feet, which in longer than that of a Boeing 777 aircraft (which is 212 feet).

The International Space Station weighs almost one million pounds (actually about 925,000 lbs.) which is the equivalent of the weight of 320 cars all together.

Original Zarya Module

The largest part of the International Space Station is a central truss. There are sixteen huge solar panels attached to the truss, as are the modules where the astronauts live and work. The original Zarya Module is used mainly for storage and external fuel tanks.

Rear View of the Zvezda Service Module

The newer Zvezda Service module houses the crew's living quarters and the life-support systems.

International Space Station Orbiting Earth

The International Space Station travels around the Earth at an average speed of 27,700 km (or about 17,212 miles). It completes sixteen orbits each day. You can see the space station easily in the night sky as it flies 320 km (or 199 miles) above the Earth.

Working together, sixteen countries built the space station, including U.S.A., Russia, Japan, and Canada, along with other members of the ESA (European Space Agency). The Columbus science laboratory was Europe's biggest International Space Station project. Astronauts carry out scientific experiments in weightless conditions there, along with many other different types of experiments that take place both inside and outside of the science laboratory.

ATV 4 Albert Einstein Docking with Zvezda

A series of Automated Transfer Vehicles (made by the European Space Agency) carry supplies like food, fuel, and equipment to the space station. This particular ATV has been so successful that plans are now being made to design an even more advanced version that would be able to bring cargo and finished experiments back to Earth.

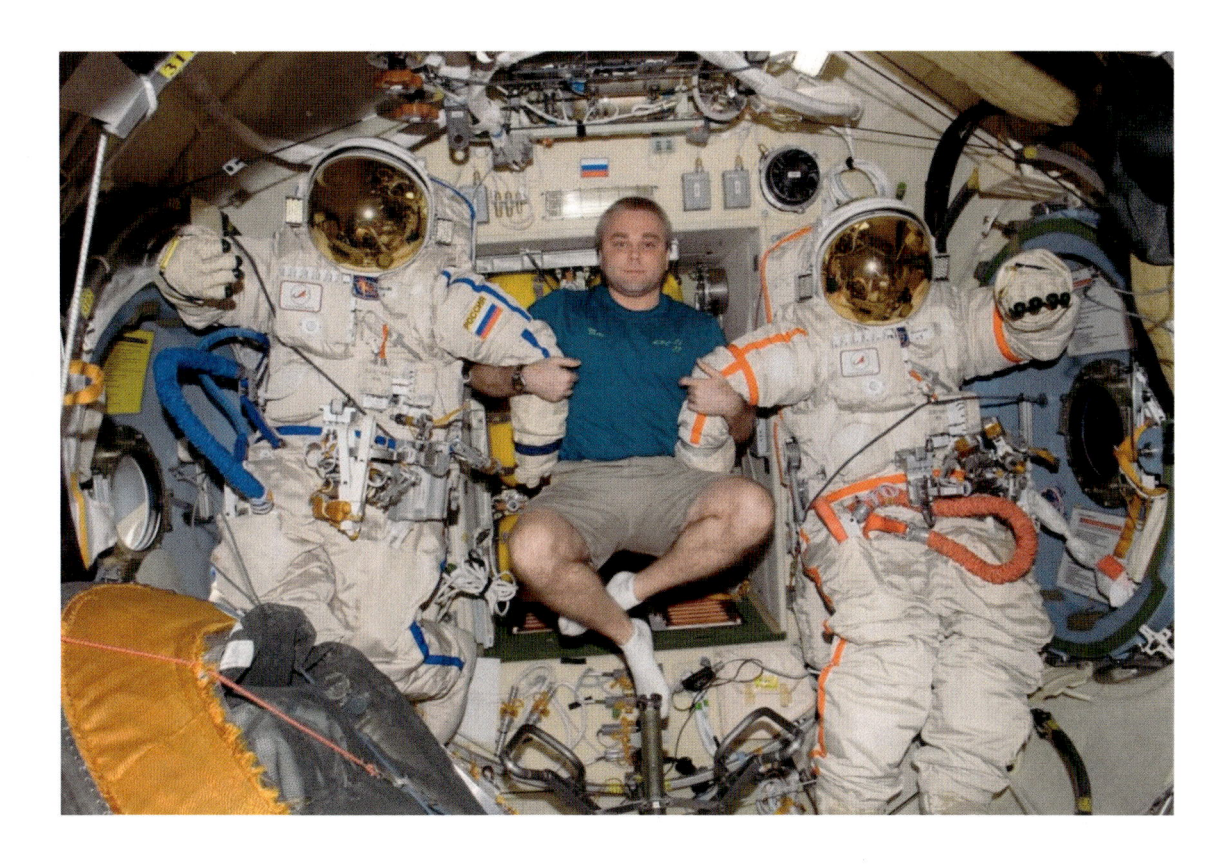

So what is living on a space station really like?

For astronauts, living on a space station is like being stranded on a desert island. The crew of two or three astronauts stationed there must survive far away from Earth for weeks and sometimes even months at a time. The astronauts must learn to live and work as a team in order for the mission to be successful. A typical term for these astronauts is six months.

Astronauts Joan Higginbotham (STS-116) and Sunita Williams (Expedition 14) on the International Space Station

ESA astronauts come from different countries and they must all learn to get along, even though they sometimes speak different languages and have only known each other for a short time before being stranded in space together. They must learn to get along with people who have different customs from themselves and that have different ways of looking at things. Sometimes the different ways of looking at things comes in handy when trying to solve any problems that may come up.

Russian Cosmonaut Nikolai Budarin in Zvezda

Astronauts living on the space station are not really out of touch with people on Earth though. Astronauts can send email and use video links to talk to their families. Also, they get regular deliveries of mail from Earth and sometimes even visiting crews.

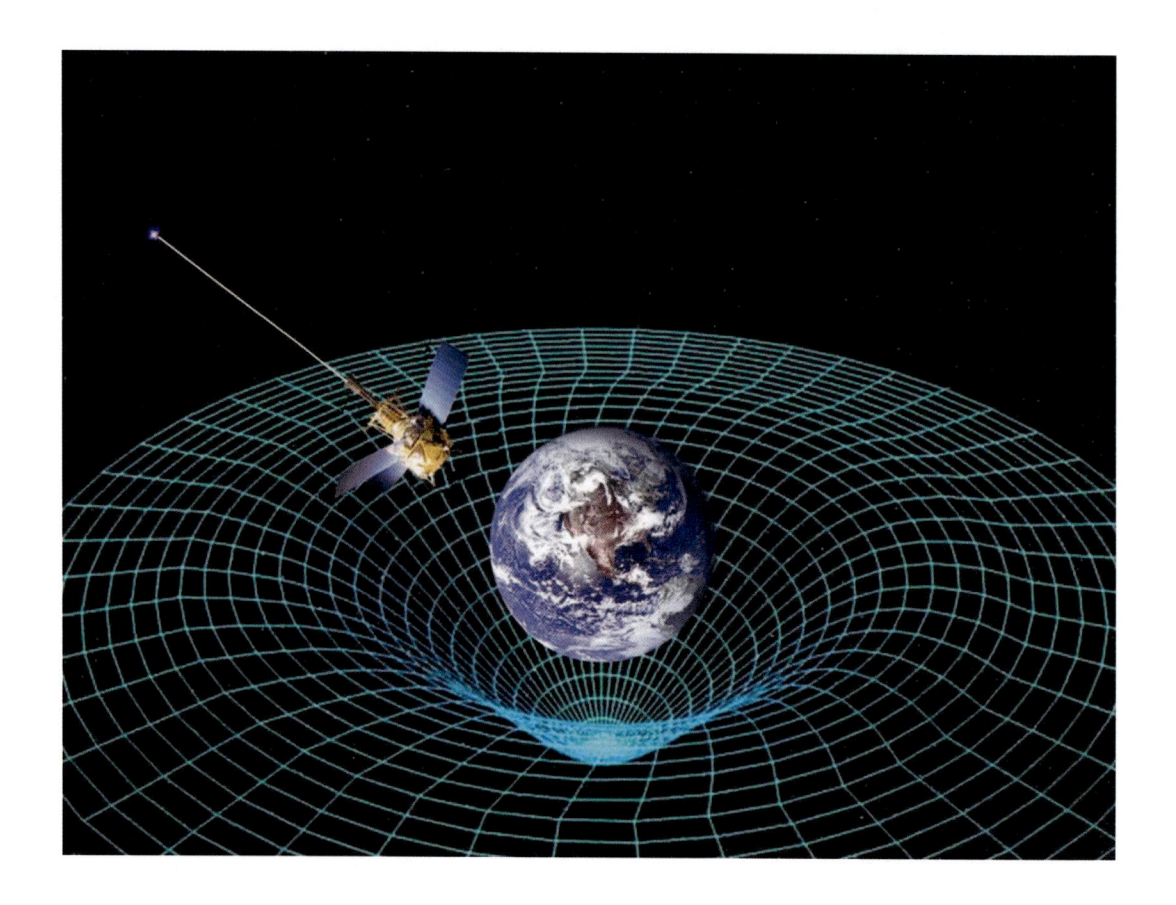

Gravity is the force that holds everything close to the planet Earth. It is a force of attraction between two objects that acts like a magnet pulling objects together and holding them down to Earth. All the trees, buildings, animals, water and even the air we breathe is held to the Earth by gravity. Without gravity things would float away to outer space.

If you were living on the space station, you would be living in a near weightless environment. If you ever take a look at a video of the space station crew, they seem to be floating about. Actually, though, a strong force of gravity (about 90% of the Earth's gravity) is placed on the ISS – but it still allows things to float around.

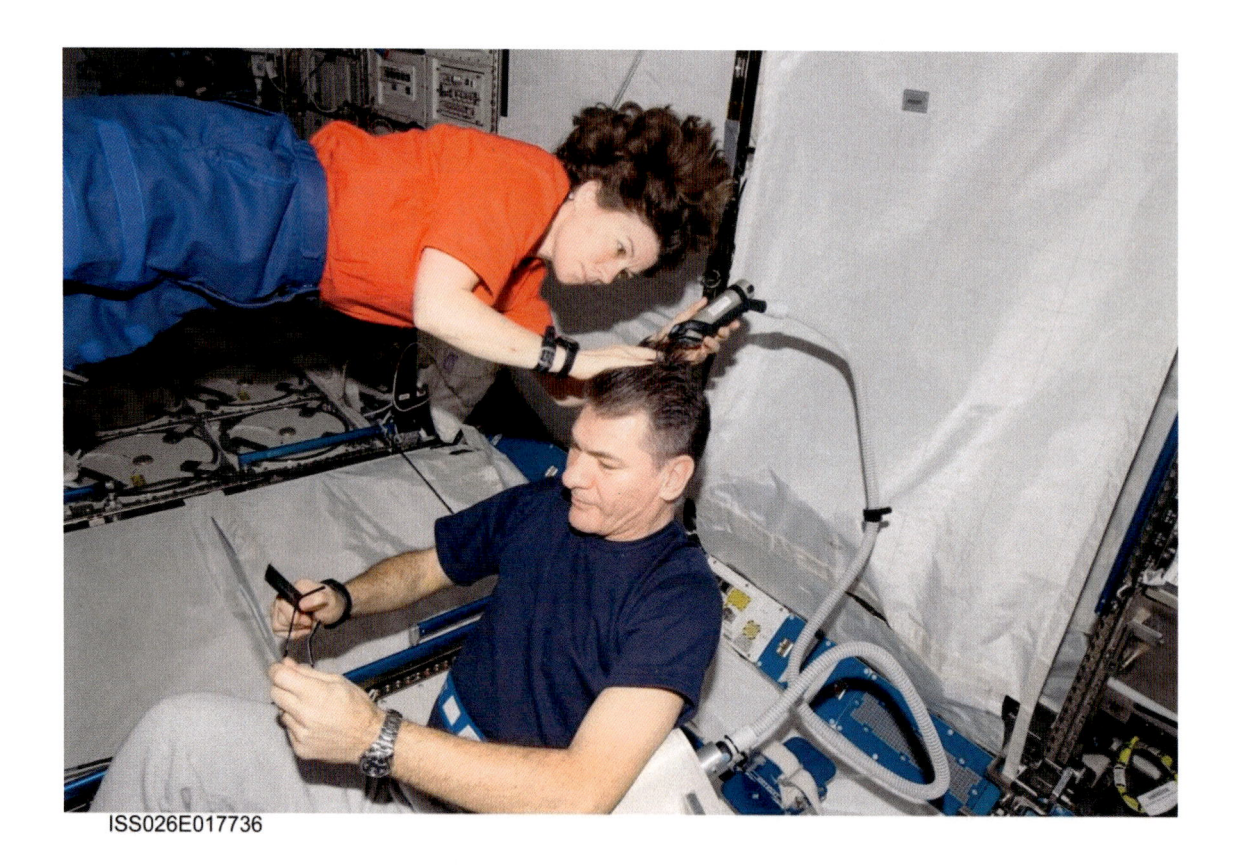

The lack of gravity in space and the lesser gravity of the space station is what allows things to float around. The astronauts seem to 'swim' in the air to get from place to place. Objects float around them. For instance, if they let go of a pencil it will stay in the air instead of falling to the floor.

The weightlessness makes it harder in some ways for the astronauts to survive in space. Their food and drinks must be served in special containers and be used in certain ways in order for the astronauts to eat and drink. They must use special equipment to go to the bathroom even.

In the 1960's when astronauts traveled to outer space, bite-sized food was placed in aluminum tubes. The food the astronauts in space eat now has improved since then. Now, the meals the astronauts eat are very similar to the meals we eat here on Earth. The food is placed in plastic containers. Some space foods need to have hot or cold water added to them when they are heated up in the oven. Although fruits, bread and nuts can be eaten as they are, liquid drinks must be sucked up through a straw stuck in a sealed package.

Helen Sharman in her space suit

Before, astronauts in space suits had to have special tubing to hook up to in order for them to go to the bathroom. On board the International Space Station, although there are no wash basins or showers, the toilet looks similar to the ones on Earth. Because of the low gravity, the astronauts must sit correctly on the toilet and fasten their bodies to it by suction so they won't float away. A vacuum-cleaner-like machine sucks up their waste and the waste is then vacuum-dried.

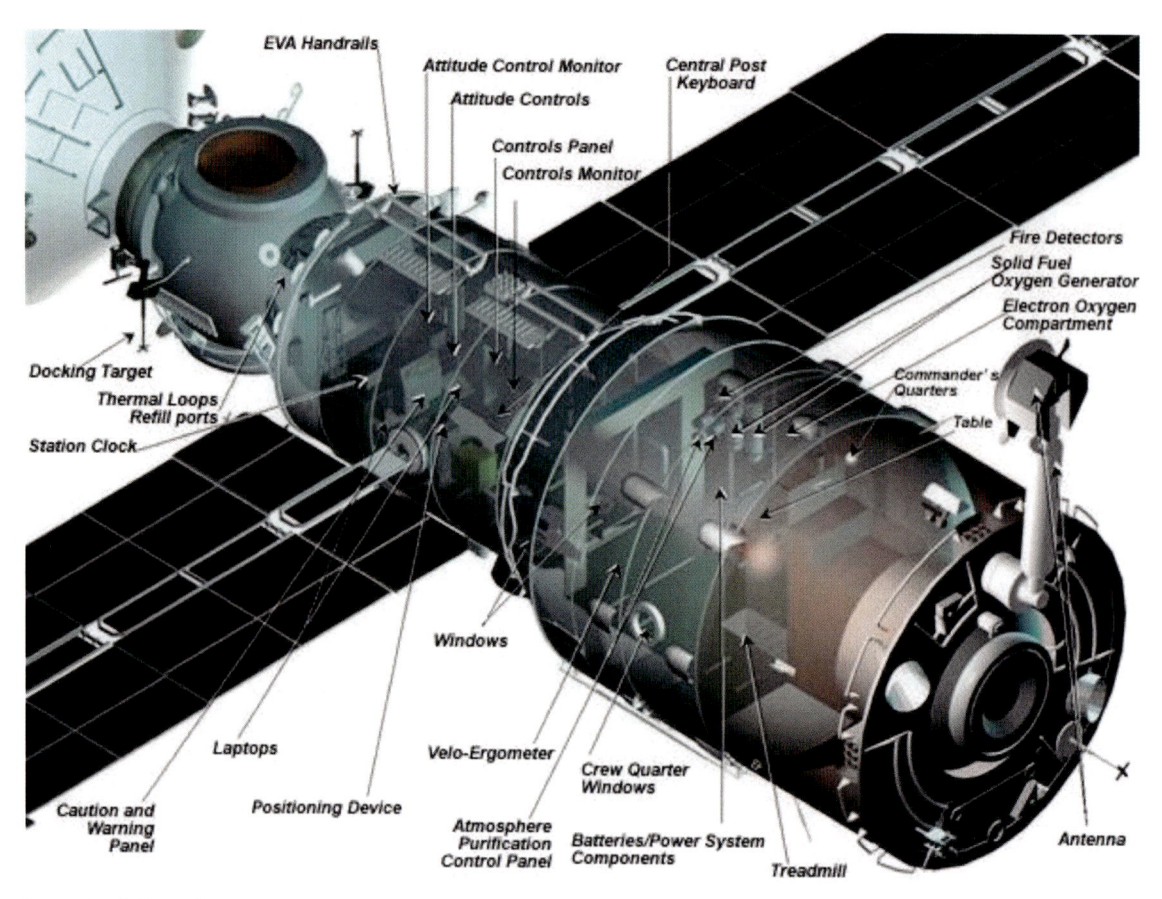

Layout of Zvezda

A curtain separates the toilet space from the rest of the living space. Because there is no door, the astronauts can all hear the sounds coming from inside the toilet space. But, because there are a lot of noises from other machinery, it is not as noisy as you might think.

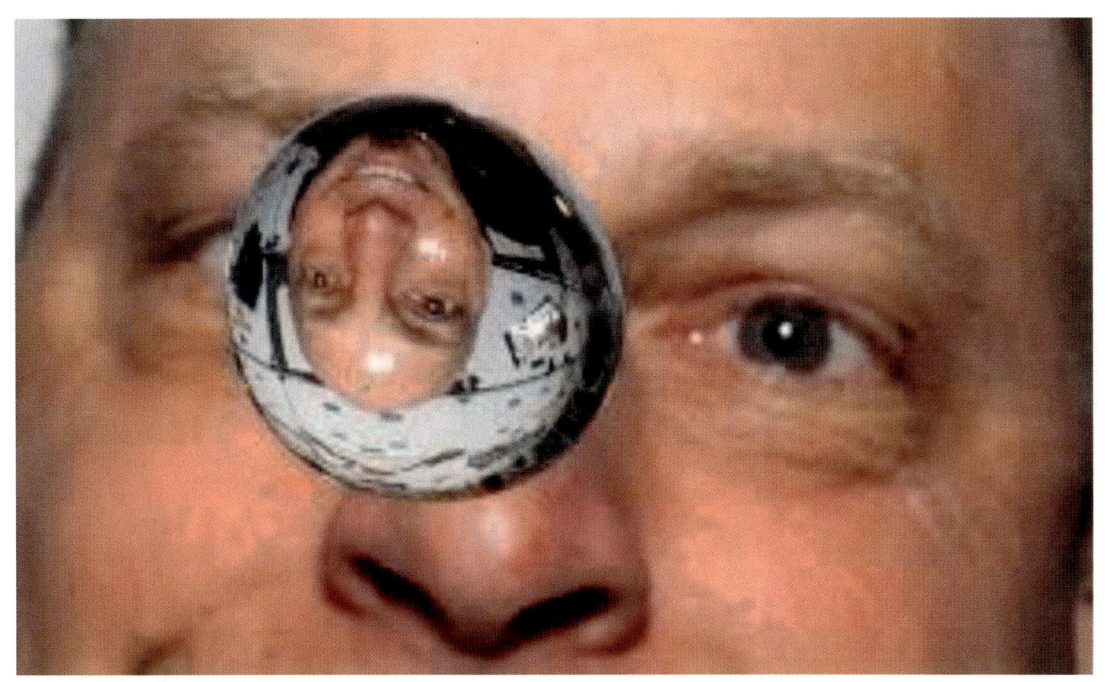

Water drop floating in space

Since water cannot flow in low gravity, the astronauts cannot shower or wash their hands under a water tap as you do on Earth. They must clean themselves using alcohol or by using a wet towel containing liquid soap. The astronauts simply wipe themselves all over using a wet towel soaked with body shampoo. They use waterless shampoo to wash their hair. After washing they use dry towels to dry themselves.

Crew Lounging on ISS – Expedition 35 Commander Chris Hadfield of the Canadian Space Agency (at right), Clockwise from his position are the 5 flight engineers – NASA Astronauts Tom Marshburn and Chris Cassidy, Russian Cosmonauts Alexander Misurkin, Roman Romanenko and Pavel Vinogradov

Space is very cold. Unlike here on Earth, the vacuum of space has no temperature. Inside the space station, the temperature is controlled though. The air pressure is kept at one atmosphere, which is the same level as here on Earth, so that the astronauts can live comfortably. The astronauts don't need any special clothing to live day-to-day. The astronauts living on the space station dress the same way we do here on Earth. Unlike here on Earth, though, astronauts cannot do their laundry like we do. The astronauts must bring several sets of clothing and underwear to change into every day.

When venturing outside the space station, astronauts must wear spacesuits. The spacesuits are high-performance suits with various functions that protect the astronaut from the vacuum of space and the harsh conditions of space. The spacesuits provide air for the astronauts to breathe and keep the temperature inside regular. The spacesuits also protect the astronauts from radiation and special face plates protect them from the sun's brightness.

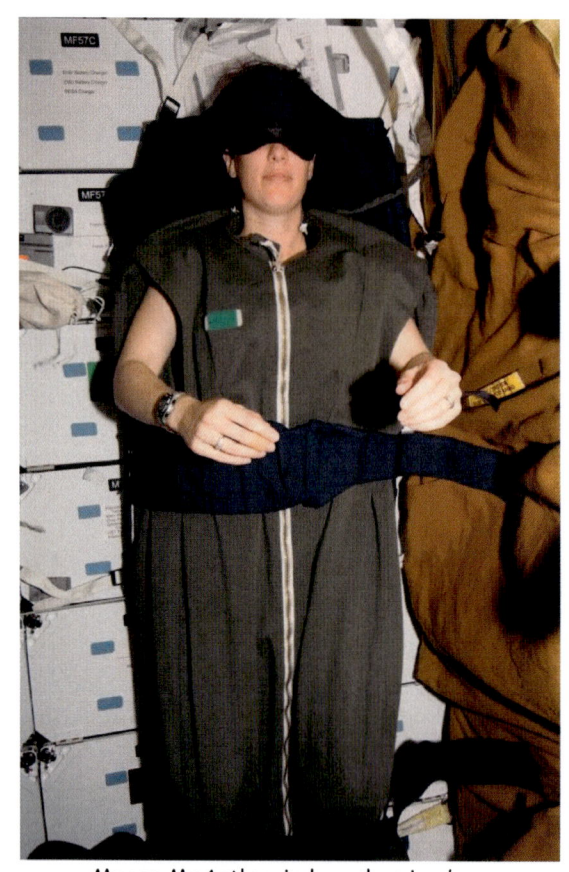

Megan McArthur in her sleeping bag

Sleeping on the space station is also different than here on Earth. Since there is no gravity, astronauts sleep in small sleeping compartments. They use sleeping bags and strap themselves loosely inside the compartment so that their bodies do not float around. Some astronauts use eye masks and ear plugs to block out the light and noise so that they can sleep. The space station schedules the astronauts to allow them to sleep eight hours per day, but usually the astronauts sleep about six hours. They work long hours or like to spend time enjoying the views in space.

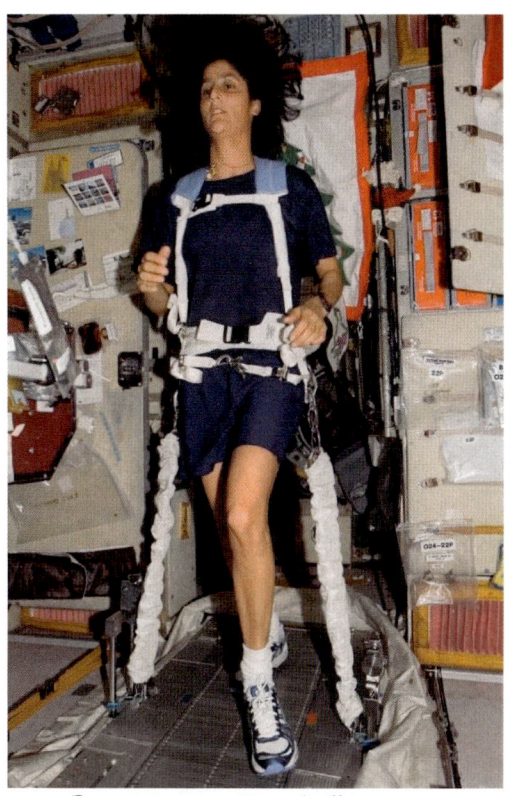

Exercising on a Treadmill in Space

Because of the gravity here on Earth, people are constantly using their muscles to fight against it, when walking or running or simply moving through everyday life. On the space station, the gravity is so low astronauts must have an exercise program to keep their bones and muscles strong. Astronauts living on the space station spend at least two hours each day exercising, on machines like a treadmill or ergometer (which is like a bicycle without wheels). They can strap their body to a treadmill and do running exercises on it, or they can bicycle using the ergometer.

Just like here on Earth, where people live the area needs to be cleaned and kept tidy. There is also garbage that needs to be disposed of. Part of an astronaut's job is to help keep the space station clean. They must change the air purification system's filters, collect the garbage (which is brought back to Earth), and clean the eating area, the walls and the floors. They use liquid detergent, disposable plastic gloves, multi-purpose wiping cloths and vacuum cleaners for cleaning.

Living on the space station is not all work. Astronauts have time for fun and their own activities too. Astronauts are allowed to bring certain belongings from home, including books and music. They can watch DVD movies too. Once a week, they are allowed to talk to their families back on Earth.

International Space Station Crew – NASA Astronauts Steve Bowen, Nicole Stott, both STS-133 mission specialists, Steve Lindsey, STS-133 Commander, European Space Agency' Astronaut Paolo Nespoli, Expedition 26, Expedition 26 Flight Engineer and NASA Astronaut Michael Barratt, STS-133 mission specialist.

The astronaut crew aboard the space station is occupied with a full agenda of scientific experiments and research. The primary fields of research conducted on the space station include human research (the effects of weightlessness on the human body), space medicine, life sciences (the study of living organisms – micro-organisms, humans, plants and animals), physical sciences (the study of physics and chemistry), astronomy (the study of celestial bodies like planets, moons, star, nebulae and galaxies) sand meteorology (the study of the atmosphere and weather).

Being an astronaut and living on the International Space Station takes a special kind of person. First of all, you have to pass the entire astronaut training in order to go into space. Then you have to be able to withstand living with others in close quarters and small places. You have to be able to get along very well with others. Then you have to be able to be away from your family for long periods of time.

Living on a space station isn't for everyone. But the rewards are plenty. Image seeing Earth from outer space. Image looking out of your window and seeing all the stars and the moon close-up. Image doing research and being the first person to discover a new star or comet. Space is a beautiful place. There are endless possibilities.

If you liked this book, you may also like:

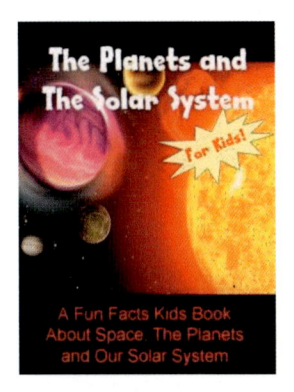

The Planets and The Solar System: A Fun Facts Book About The Planets and Our Solar System

Available on Amazon at:
http://www.amazon.com/dp/B00E1PJE1Q

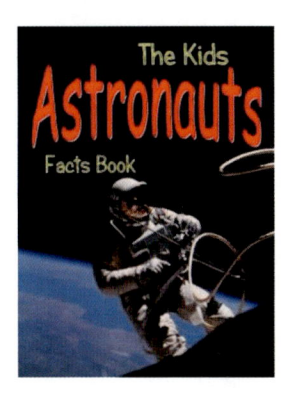

The Kids Astronauts Facts Book

Available on Amazon at:
http://www.amazon.com/dp/B00E54VPUQ

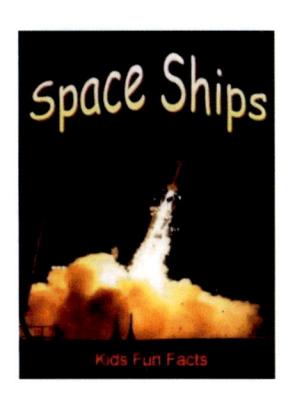

Space Ships: A Kids Book About Spacecraft and Traveling to Outer Space

Available on Amazon at:
http://www.amazon.com/dp/B00ED1ZBKG

Landmark Press Publishing

Made in the USA
Columbia, SC
09 October 2020